Success With

Grammar

SCHOLASTIC

Editor: Ourania Papacharalambous
Cover design by Tannaz Fassihi; cover illustration by Kevin Zimmer
Interior design by Mina Chen
Interior illustrations by Pauline Reeves (7–9, 11, 14, 16–17, 20, 22, 25, 29, 31, 33–37, 42, 44-45); Doug Jones (3, 6, 18, 19, 24, 27); Rusty Fletcher (23, 26, 32, 35, 40, 41)
All other images © Shutterstock.com

ISBN 978-1-338-79839-5
Scholastic Inc., 557 Broadway, New York, NY 10012
Copyright © 2022 Scholastic Inc.
All rights reserved. Printed in the U.S.A.
First printing, January 2022
1 2 3 4 5 6 7 8 9 10   40   29 28 27 26 25 24 23 22

INTRODUCTION

No other resource boosts grammar skills like *Scholastic Success With Grammar*! For classroom or at-home use, this exciting series for grades 1 through 5 provides invaluable reinforcement and practice in grammar topics such as sentence types, verb tenses, parts of speech, subject-verb agreement, common and proper nouns, punctuation, sentence structure, capitalization, contractions, and more!

This 48-page book contains loads of clever practice pages to keep kids challenged and excited as they strengthen the grammar skills they need to read and write well. On page 4, you will find a list of the key skills covered in the activities throughout this book. Each practice page reinforces a specific, age-appropriate skill. What's more, the activities for each skill are followed by an assessment sheet that gives children realistic practice in taking tests—and gives you a useful tool to follow their progress!

Take the lead and help children succeed with *Scholastic Success With Grammar*. Parents and teachers agree: No one helps children succeed like Scholastic.

TABLE OF CONTENTS

Key Skills 4

Types of Sentences; Capital *I* 5

Common Nouns 8

Capitalize Names and Places 11

Verbs 14

Simple Sentences 17

Pronouns 20

Plural Nouns 23

Adjectives 26

Verb *to be* 29

Irregular Verbs *go, do* 32

Quotation Marks 35

Contractions With *not* 38

Subject–Verb Agreement 41

Verbs *have, has, had* 44

Answer Key 47

Grade-Appropriate Skills Covered in *Scholastic Success With Grammar: Grade 2*

Know and use various text features to locate key facts or information in a text efficiently.

Know and apply grade-level phonics and word analysis skills in decoding words.

Decode regularly spelled two-syllable words with long vowels.

Decode words with common prefixes and suffixes.

Read with sufficient accuracy and fluency to support comprehension.

Demonstrate command of the conventions of standard English grammar and usage when writing or speaking.

Use collective nouns.

Use adjectives and adverbs, and choose between them depending on what is to be modified.

Demonstrate command of the conventions of standard English capitalization, punctuation, and spelling when writing.

Generalize learned spelling patterns when writing words.

Capitalize holidays, product names, and geographic names.

Use an apostrophe to form contractions and frequently occurring possessives.

Use knowledge of language and its conventions when writing, speaking, reading, or listening.

Demonstrate understanding of word relationships and nuances in word meanings.

Use words and phrases acquired through conversations, reading and being read to, and responding to texts, including using adjectives and adverbs to describe.

Types of Sentences; Capital *I*

Read each sentence. Circle the beginning letter, end punctuation, and the word *I* in each sentence.

All sentences begin with a capital letter.

A **telling sentence** ends with a period.

A **question** ends with a question mark.

An **exclamation** ends with an exclamation mark.

A **command** ends with a period or an exclamation mark.

The word *I* is always capitalized in a sentence.

1 I sail my boat in the lake.

2 May I have a turn?

3 I am so happy!

4 Can Kiku and I play?

5 Bill and I fly the kite.

Write each sentence from above in the correct box.

Telling Sentences

_____

_____

Questions

_____

_____

Exclamation _____

Types of Sentences; Capital *I*

Decide if each sentence is a telling sentence, a question, an exclamation, or a command. Write *T, Q, E,* or *C* on the lines.

1 My sister and I went to the lake. _____

2 Come see this. _____

3 I saw three little sailboats. _____

4 Put the boat in the water. _____

5 Did I have a good time? _____

6 You bet! I loved it! _____

7 Can I go again soon? _____

....

What would you do at the lake?
Use the word *I* and your own ideas to finish the sentences.

1 _____ saw _____ at the lake.

2 _____ can _____ .

3 My friend and _____ liked _____ best.

Types of Sentences; Capital *I*

Read each sentence. If it is written correctly, fill in the last bubble. If not, fill in the bubble next to the correct way to write it.

1 i have fun with my bike.
- ○ I have fun with my bike.
- ○ I have fun with my bike
- ○ i have fun with my bike
- ○ correct as is

2 can I ride to the beach
- ○ Can I ride to the beach
- ○ Can I ride to the beach?
- ○ Can i ride to the beach?
- ○ correct as is

3 i found a pretty shell
- ○ I found a pretty shell
- ○ i found a pretty shell.
- ○ I found a pretty shell.
- ○ correct as is

4 Jill and I see a crab.
- ○ Jill and I see a crab
- ○ Jill and i see a crab.
- ○ Jill and i see a crab
- ○ correct as is

5 get the shovel
- ○ Get the shovel
- ○ Get the shovel.
- ○ get the shovel.
- ○ correct as is

6 what a mess I made
- ○ What a mess I made!
- ○ What a mess I made
- ○ what a mess I made!
- ○ correct as is

Common Nouns

Common nouns name people, places, animals, or things.

Read each sentence. Circle the common nouns.

1 The boy made a boat.

2 The brothers walked their dog.

3 A girl was with her grandmother.

4 Two boats crashed in the lake.

5 Friends used a needle and thread to fix the sail.

Write the common nouns you circled under the correct heading below.

People	Places	Things

Animals

Common Nouns

Complete each sentence about the picture.
Use the nouns in the Word Bank below.

Word Bank

| bench | bridge | carousel | children | stream | swing |

1. The _____ is near the tree.

2. The _____ is beside the slide.

3. The _____ are playing in the park.

4. The _____ is near a bush.

5. The _____ is over the stream.

6. The _____ runs through the park.

Common Nouns

Look at the underlined word in each sentence.
If it is a common noun, fill in the bubble next to *yes*.
If it is not a common noun, fill in the bubble next to *no*.

1 Our class <u>went</u> on a trip.
   ◯ yes   ◯ no

2 We went to the <u>city</u>.
   ◯ yes   ◯ no

3 The buildings were <u>tall</u>.
   ◯ yes   ◯ no

4 There were many <u>cars</u>.
   ◯ yes   ◯ no

- -

A common noun is underlined in each sentence. Tell if it names a person, place, animal, or thing. Fill in the bubble next to the correct answer.

1 We went into a big <u>room</u>.
   ◯ person   ◯ place   ◯ animal   ◯ thing

2 Our <u>teacher</u> led us.
   ◯ person   ◯ place   ◯ animal   ◯ thing

3 I walked with my best <u>friend</u>.
   ◯ person   ◯ place   ◯ animal   ◯ thing

4 We sat at a long <u>table</u>.
   ◯ person   ◯ place   ◯ animal   ◯ thing

5 My dog and <u>cat</u> are best friends.
   ◯ person   ◯ place   ◯ animal   ◯ thing

Capitalize Names and Places

Special names of people, animals, and places always begin with capital letters. They are called **proper nouns**.

Read each sentence. Circle the proper noun.

1. George Ancona loves history.

2. His parents were born in Mexico.

3. His family calls him Jorgito.

4. They live on Coney Island.

5. They have a pet bird named Pilar.

6. Tio Mario works in a sign shop.

Write the proper nouns you circled under the correct heading below.

People	Animals	Places

Capitalize Names and Places

Read the postcard. Find the proper nouns.
Write them correctly on the lines below.

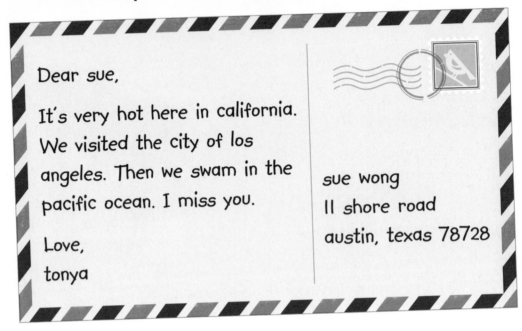

Dear sue,

It's very hot here in california.
We visited the city of los
angeles. Then we swam in the
pacific ocean. I miss you.

Love,
tonya

sue wong
11 shore road
austin, texas 78728

1 _____

2 _____

3 _____

4 _____

5 _____

6 _____

7 _____

8 _____

Write a sentence with a proper noun. Underline the capital letter or letters
in the proper noun. Then write whether it names a person or a place.

_____

_____

Capitalize Names and Places

A proper noun is underlined in each sentence. Does it name a person, animal, or place? Fill in the bubble next to the correct answer.

1 <u>Betty</u> is a photographer.
- ○ person
- ○ animal
- ○ place

2 She goes to <u>Florida</u> to take pictures.
- ○ person
- ○ animal
- ○ place

3 She takes her dog <u>Rex</u> with her.
- ○ person
- ○ animal
- ○ place

4 She takes his picture in a city called <u>Miami</u>.
- ○ person
- ○ animal
- ○ place

• •

Read each sentence. Find the proper noun.
Fill in the bubble next to the word that is a proper noun.

1 Their friend is Emilio.
- ○ friend
- ○ Emilio
- ○ Their
- ○ is

2 They all went to Orlando.
- ○ Orlando
- ○ all
- ○ They
- ○ went

3 They visited Disney World there.
- ○ They
- ○ there
- ○ visited
- ○ Disney World

4 They walked down Main Street in the park.
- ○ park
- ○ walked
- ○ They
- ○ Main Street

Verbs

Read each sentence. Write the action verb in the telling part of the sentence.

> A **verb** is an action word. It tells what someone or something is doing.

1 Ronald runs to the field. _____

2 Michael wears a batting helmet. _____

3 He smacks the ball hard. _____

4 Ronald holds the wrong end of the bat. _____

5 He misses the ball. _____

6 Ronald waits in left field. _____

7 He writes *G* for great. _____

8 Ronald's father helps him. _____

· ·

Write a sentence about the picture. Use an action verb and circle it.

_____

_____

_____

Verbs

**Find the past-tense verb in each sentence.
Write it on the line.**

> Some verbs add **-ed** to tell about actions that happened in the past.

1 Last spring, Daisy planted a garden. _____

2 Floyd watered the garden. _____

3 Together they weeded their garden. _____

4 One day, they discovered a big carrot. _____

· ·

**Read each sentence. If the sentence has a present-tense verb, write
present on the line. If the sentence has a past-tense verb, write *past*
on the line.**

1 They like to eat carrots. _____

2 They pulled on the carrot. _____

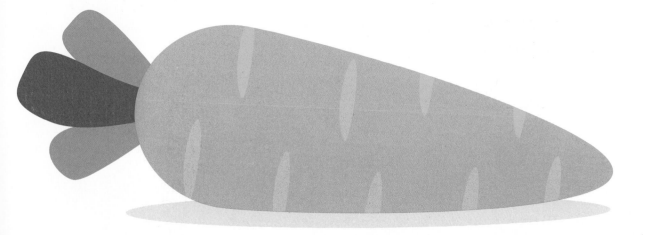

Verbs

Look at the underlined verb in each sentence.
Fill in the correct bubble to tell whether or not it is an action verb.

1 The dog <u>runs</u> down the road.
○ action verb
○ not an action verb

2 The dog hides <u>under</u> a bush.
○ action verb
○ not an action verb

3 The <u>sun</u> sets.
○ action verb
○ not an action verb

4 The girl <u>sees</u> a rainbow.
○ action verb
○ not an action verb

. . . .

Look at the underlined verb in each sentence. If it is not correct, fill in the bubble next to the correct verb. If it is correct, fill in the last bubble.

1 Yesterday, the girl <u>chased</u> the dog.
○ chase
○ correct as is

2 It <u>rain</u> last night.
○ rained
○ correct as is

Simple Sentences

Read each group of words. Put an *X* next to it if it is a complete thought. Circle the naming part and underline the telling part in each sentence.

1 One day thirsty   _____

2 Crow could not get a drink.   _____

3 The water rose.   _____

4 The old mouse   _____

5 Put the bell   _____

6 One mouse had a plan.   _____

Write a simple sentence about the picture below.
Circle the naming part and underline the telling part.

_____

Simple Sentences

Circle the sentence in each pair.
Then underline the naming part of the sentence.

1 Lin likes to play soccer.

likes to play soccer

2 Her friends

Her friends watch her play.

3 They cheer for Lin.

They cheer for

4 Her mom goes to
all of her games.

goes to all of her games

5 The coach is very proud of Lin.

The coach is

6 plays tennis on Saturdays

Elijah plays tennis
on Saturdays.

7 The bird built a nest.

built a nest

8 Sara and Simeon
baked a cake.

baked a cake

Simple Sentences

Read each sentence. Fill in the bubble to tell if the underlined words are the naming or the telling part of the sentence. Some of the underlined words may not be the whole part.

1 The cat <u>was under the tree.</u>
- ○ naming part
- ○ telling part
- ○ not the whole part

3 The bird <u>flew</u> away.
- ○ naming part
- ○ telling part
- ○ not the whole part

2 <u>A bird</u> saw the cat.
- ○ naming part
- ○ telling part
- ○ not the whole part

4 <u>Then, the</u> cat walked away.
- ○ naming part
- ○ telling part
- ○ not the whole part

Fill in the bubble to choose a naming or telling part that makes a sentence.

1 The bird ____.
- ○ in the tall tree
- ○ saw the cat go away
- ○ flying very fast in the sky

3 ____ saw the bird.
- ○ After a minute, the cat
- ○ Running across the grass
- ○ The cat was watching

2 ____ came back to the tree.
- ○ Deep in the woods
- ○ The large and pretty
- ○ Then, the bird

4 So the cat ____.
- ○ walking to the tree
- ○ under the tree
- ○ walked back, too

Pronouns

Read each pair of sentences. Circle the pronoun in the second sentence of each pair. Then, write what the pronoun stands for. The first one has been done for you.

> **A pronoun** takes the place of the name of a person, place, animal, or thing.

1 Wendell did not like to clean his room.

(He) liked a messy room.   Wendell

2 Mom wanted Wendell to do some work.

She handed Wendell a broom.   _____

3 The pigs came into Wendell's room.

They helped Wendell clean the room.   _____

4 Wendell and the pigs played a board game.

Wendell and the pigs had fun playing it.   _____

5 The pigs and Wendell played for a long time.

They liked to play games.   _____

6 Wendell was sad to see his friends go.

He liked playing with the pigs.   _____

Pronouns

Read the story. Use the pronouns below to complete the paragraph. The first one has been done for you. Remember, every sentence should begin with a capital letter.

they	he	she	it

Glenda was walking in the woods. At last _she_

came to a house. _____ was empty. She opened the
                        1

door and saw three chairs by the fireplace. _____
                                              2

were all different sizes. She sat down in the smallest one.

_____ was the perfect size for her. Soon _____
3   **4**

fell asleep. When she woke up, three pigs were

standing over her. The father pig spoke. _____
                                           5

asked Glenda if she would stay for dinner. "I would love to!"

said Glenda.

Pronouns

Read each sentence. Fill in the bubble next to the word or words that the underlined pronoun stands for.

1 She did not like the mess.
- ○ Wendell
- ○ The boy
- ○ The pigs
- ○ Ms. Fultz

2 He did not like brooms.
- ○ The pigs
- ○ The boys
- ○ The boy
- ○ Ms. Fultz

3 It was full of pigs.
- ○ The rooms
- ○ The house
- ○ The pigs
- ○ The door

4 They wanted to play.
- ○ The room
- ○ Wendell
- ○ The pigs
- ○ Mrs. Fultz

Read each sentence. Fill in the bubble next to the pronoun that can take the place of the underlined word or words.

1 Wendell waved goodbye to the pigs.
- ○ He
- ○ She
- ○ It
- ○ They

2 Wendell hoped the pigs would come back.
- ○ it
- ○ he
- ○ they
- ○ she

Plural Nouns

**Read the sentences. Underline the plural nouns.
Circle the letter or letters that were added to
mean more than one.**

Most nouns add
-s to mean more
than one. Nouns
that end in **s, x,
ch,** or **sh** add **-es**
to mean more
than one.

1 We have two accordions
in our house.

2 Grandma has many
brushes to fix her hair.

3 My grandfather has many
clocks and watches.

4 A lot of flowers are in the boxes.

. . . .

Write the nouns that added _-s._

_____

Write the nouns that added _-es._

_____

Plural Nouns

Read each sentence. Add *-s* or *-es* to the noun at the end of the sentence to make it plural. Write it in the sentence.

1 Dad made five cheese _____. (sandwich)

2 He packed five _____ for the children. (meal)

3 Lisa put fruit in all the _____. (lunchbox)

4 She packed some paper _____, too. (plate)

. . . .

Write the plural for each noun on the line.

1 one box

two _____

2 one dress

two _____

3 one coat

two _____

4 one bench

two _____

Plural Nouns

Read each pair of nouns.
If the plural noun is correct, fill in the last bubble.
If it is not correct, fill in the bubble next to the correct plural noun.

1 sketch, sketchs
○ sketches
○ correct as is

5 tree, trees
○ treess
○ correct as is

2 fox, foxs
○ foxes
○ correct as is

6 paint, paints
○ paintes
○ correct as is

3 squirrel, squirrels
○ squirreles
○ correct as is

7 dress, dressees
○ dresses
○ correct as is

4 ball, balles
○ balls
○ correct as is

8 wish, wishes
○ wishs
○ correct as is

Adjectives

**Read each sentence. Underline the nouns.
Write the adjective that tells about each noun.**

> An **adjective** describes a person, place, animal, or thing. Color, size, and number words are adjectives.

1 The brown donkey carried the heavy sack.

_____   _____

2 The striped cat chased two birds.

_____   _____

3 The little rooster crowed six times.

_____   _____

- -

Write the adjectives from the sentences above.

1 Write the adjectives that tell what kind.

_____

2 Write the adjectives that tell how many.

_____

Adjectives

Read each sentence. Find the adjective and the noun it describes.
Circle the noun. Write the adjective on the line.

1 Peggy and Rosa went to a big animal sanctuary. _____

2 They looked up at the tall giraffe. _____

3 The giraffe looked down at the two girls. _____

4 The giraffe had brown spots. _____

Write adjectives from the sentences in the chart.

Color Word

Size Words

Number Word

Adjectives

Read each sentence. Fill in the bubble next to the word that is an adjective.

1 In the morning,
Jenny put on red boots.
- ○ put
- ○ red
- ○ boots
- ○ on

2 She found a yellow hat
in the closet.
- ○ She
- ○ hat
- ○ found
- ○ yellow

3 She opened her
purple umbrella.
- ○ opened
- ○ She
- ○ umbrella
- ○ purple

4 Jenny walked past
a big house.
- ○ big
- ○ house
- ○ walked
- ○ past

5 She waved to three friends.
- ○ waved
- ○ three
- ○ to
- ○ friends

6 A little puppy trotted
behind her.
- ○ trotted
- ○ puppy
- ○ little
- ○ behind

7 She jumped over
a huge puddle.
- ○ She
- ○ huge
- ○ jumped
- ○ puddle

8 Two birds took
a drink of water.
- ○ birds
- ○ of
- ○ took
- ○ Two

Verb *to be*

Read each sentence. Underline the verb.
Write *past* if the sentence tells about the past.
Write *present* if the sentence tells about the present.

Am, is, are, was, and **were** are forms of the verb *to be*. These verbs show being instead of action.

1 The story is perfect. _____

2 The producers are happy. _____

3 The actors were funny. _____

4 The movie studio is interested in the story. _____

5 I am excited about the movie. _____

6 I was sad at the end. _____

Verb *to be*

Choose a verb from the Word Bank to finish each sentence. There may be more than one right answer and all words may not be used. Write *one* if the sentence tells about one. Write *more* if it tells about more than one.

Word Bank

am	is	are	was	were

1 The movie _____ long. _____

2 She _____ in the movie. _____

3 They _____ at the movie theater yesterday. _____

4 The producers _____ spending money now. _____

5 The director _____ not at work yesterday. _____

6 The actors _____ acting now. _____

Verb *to be*

Read each sentence. Fill in the bubble next to the words that correctly tell about the sentence.

1 The movie was very long.
- ○ past, more than one
- ○ present, more than one
- ○ past, one
- ○ present, one

2 The seats at the movies are high up.
- ○ past, more than one
- ○ present, more than one
- ○ past, one
- ○ present, one

3 The actors were all big stars.
- ○ past, more than one
- ○ present, more than one
- ○ past, one
- ○ present, one

4 The scenes were interesting.
- ○ past, more than one
- ○ present, more than one
- ○ past, one
- ○ present, one

5 The locations used in the movie were so beautiful.
- ○ past, more than one
- ○ present, more than one
- ○ past, one
- ○ present, one

6 I am going to see the movie again.
- ○ past, more than one
- ○ present, more than one
- ○ past, one
- ○ present, one

Irregular Verbs *go, do*

Read each sentence. Write *present* if the underlined verb tells about action now. Write *past* if it tells about action in the past.

Irregular verbs change their spelling when they tell about the past. **Did** is the past form of **do** and **does**. **Went** is the past form of **go** and **goes**.

In the Present	In the Past
go, goes	went
do, does	did

1. Grace <u>goes</u> to the playground. _____

2. Some other children <u>go</u>, too. _____

3. Grace <u>does</u> a scene from a story. _____

4. The children <u>do</u> the scene with her. _____

5. Grace <u>went</u> into battle as Joan of Arc. _____

6. She <u>did</u> the part of Anansi the Spider, too. _____

7. In another part, Grace <u>went</u> inside a wooden horse. _____

8. She <u>did</u> many other parts. _____

Irregular Verbs *go, do*

Choose the correct word from the chart and write it on the line.

In the Present	In the Past
go, goes	went
do, does	did

1 Last week our family _____ to the art museum.

2 Pablo _____ there a lot.

3 His mother _____ the displays there now.

4 She _____ a new one yesterday.

5 _____ you want to join us tomorrow?

6 We want to _____ after lunch again.

Irregular Verbs *go, do*

Fill in the bubble next to the word that correctly completes the sentence.

1 Rose _____ to the ballet.
- ○ go
- ○ did
- ○ goes

2 Two dancers _____ a kick and a turn.
- ○ do
- ○ does
- ○ goes

3 Another dancer _____ a hop and a jump.
- ○ went
- ○ does
- ○ do

4 They _____ around in circles very fast.
- ○ goes
- ○ did
- ○ go

5 A dancer _____ two big splits.
- ○ do
- ○ did
- ○ went

6 Then she _____ off stage.
- ○ go
- ○ did
- ○ went

7 Rose _____ home feeling very happy.
- ○ went
- ○ did
- ○ go

8 She _____ some of the steps, too.
- ○ do
- ○ did
- ○ goes

Quotation Marks

Read each sentence. Underline the exact words the speaker says. Put the words in quotation marks. The first one is done for you.

> **Quotation marks** show the exact words someone says. They go before the speaker's first word. They also go after the speaker's last word and the end punctuation mark.

1. Max said, "Let's go on a picnic."

2. Cori replied,   That's a great idea.

3. Andy asked,   What should we bring?

4. Max said with a laugh,   We should bring food.

5. Cori added,   Yes, let's bring lots and lots of food.

6. Andy giggled and said,   You're no help at all!

. . . .

Finish the sentences below by writing what Max, Cori, and Andy might say next. Use quotation marks.

1. Max said, _____.

2. Cori asked, _____.

3. Andy answered, _____.

Quotation Marks

**Read the sentences. Then put quotation marks where they belong.
The first one has been done for you.**

1 Jan cried, "It's raining!"

2 She asked,   What will we do today?

3 Tomas answered,   We could read.

4 Tomas whispered,   Maybe the sun will come out soon.

5 Jan whined,   But what will we do now?

6 Tomas said,   Use your imagination!

Finish the sentence below. Use quotation marks to show what Jan asked.

Jan asked,_____

_____

Quotation Marks

Fill in the bubble next to the correct way to write the sentence.

1 ○ Let's make a sandcastle, said Lenny.

○ "Let's make a sandcastle, said Lenny.

○ "Let's make a sandcastle," said Lenny.

2 ○ Where's the pail and shovel?" asked Sonya.

○ "Where's the pail and shovel?" asked Sonya.

○ Where's the pail and shovel? asked Sonya.

3 ○ Sara said, "Maybe Otis can help."

○ Sara said, Maybe Otis can help."

○ Sara said, "Maybe Otis can help.

4 ○ Do you want to dig? asked Lenny.

○ "Do you want to dig? asked Lenny.

○ "Do you want to dig?" asked Lenny.

5 ○ Sonya shouted, Get some water!

○ Sonya shouted, "Get some water!

○ Sonya shouted, "Get some water!"

6 ○ Look what we made! cried the children.

○ "Look what we made!" cried the children.

○ Look what we made!" cried the children.

Contractions With *not*

Read each sentence.
Underline the contraction.
Write the two words the
contraction is made from.

> A **contraction** is two words made into one word. An apostrophe takes the place of the missing letter or letters. In a contraction, **not** becomes **n't**.

1. The little old man and little old woman aren't ready. _____

2. The Gingerbread Man doesn't want to be eaten. _____

3. They can't catch him. _____

4. They couldn't run fast enough. _____

5. He didn't come back. _____

6. The Gingerbread Man isn't afraid of the fox. _____

· ·

Draw a line to match each contraction to the two words it is made from.

1. hadn't   were not

2. don't   had not

3. weren't   do not

Contractions With *not*

Read each sentence. Write a contraction for the underlined words.

1 Cindy and Ed <u>could not</u> bake a cake. _____

2 There <u>was not</u> enough flour. _____

3 They <u>are not</u> happy. _____

4 They <u>cannot</u> surprise José. _____

5 <u>Do not</u> give up. _____

6 They <u>did not</u> give up. They made cupcakes! _____

. . . .

Write a sentence using a contraction you wrote.

_____

_____

Contractions With *not*

Fill in the bubble next to the contraction that correctly completes the sentence.

1 Our players ____ as big as theirs.
- ○ doesn't
- ○ haven't
- ○ aren't

2 Our coach ____ worried.
- ○ isn't
- ○ didn't
- ○ can't

3 They ____ run as fast as we can.
- ○ weren't
- ○ can't
- ○ wasn't

4 Their runners ____ tagged first base.
- ○ doesn't
- ○ haven't
- ○ isn't

5 Their hitters ____ hit the ball hard.
- ○ isn't
- ○ weren't
- ○ don't

6 Our hitters ____ miss any balls.
- ○ doesn't
- ○ didn't
- ○ aren't

7 The other players ____ catch our balls.
- ○ couldn't
- ○ haven't
- ○ isn't

8 They ____ ready for us.
- ○ don't
- ○ hadn't
- ○ weren't

© Scholastic Inc.

Subject–Verb Agreement

Read each sentence. Underline the word in parentheses ( ) that correctly completes it. Write the word on the line.

> If the naming part of a sentence names one, add **-s** to the action word. If the naming part names more than one, do not add **-s** to the action word.

1 Kim _____ a story about a monkey. (write, writes)

2 The monkey _____ his friend in the city. (meet, meets)

3 The two friends _____ on the bus. (ride, rides)

4 The monkeys _____ for toys and presents. (shop, shops)

5 The store _____ at 7 o'clock. (close, closes)

6 The monkeys _____ the time. (forget, forgets)

7 The owner _____ the door. (lock, locks)

8 The friends _____ on the window. (bang, bangs)

9 Many people _____ for help. (call, calls)

10 Finally, the monkeys _____ the door open. (hear, hears)

Subject–Verb Agreement

Read each sentence. Circle the action word in parentheses ( ) that correctly completes the sentence.

1 Two baby llamas (play/plays) in the mountains.

2 One baby llama (hide/hides) under a bush.

3 The baby animals (chase/chases) flying leaves.

4 Soon the mother llama (call/calls) them.

5 The babies (run/runs) to her.

6 The two babies (stand/stands) next to their mother.

7 One baby (close/closes) its eyes.

8 The mother llama (nudge/nudges) the baby gently.

9 But the baby llama (sleep/sleeps).

10 Soon both baby llamas (sleep/sleeps).

Subject–Verb Agreement

Fill in the bubble next to the word that correctly completes the sentence.

1. Two friends ____ beautiful bead necklaces.
   ○ make
   ○ makes

2. One girl ____ some pieces of string.
   ○ cut
   ○ cuts

3. The girls ____ red, blue, and yellow beads.
   ○ use
   ○ uses

4. The yellow beads ____ in the dark.
   ○ glow
   ○ glows

5. The necklaces ____ from the rod.
   ○ hang
   ○ hangs

6. The boys ____ necklaces for their mother.
   ○ buy
   ○ buys

7. One boy ____ the short necklace with round beads.
   ○ pick
   ○ picks

8. The other boy ____ the necklace with square beads.
   ○ pick
   ○ picks

9. Two sisters ____ the same red necklace.
   ○ wear
   ○ wears

10. The girls ____ all the necklaces.
    ○ sell
    ○ sells

Verbs *have, has, had*

Read each sentence. Write *have, has,* or *had* on the line in the sentence. Then write *present* or *past* on the line at the end to show if the sentence takes place now or in the past.

> The verb **have** is irregular. Use **have** or **has** to tell about the present. Use **had** to tell about the past.

1 The man _____ many people in his restaurant last week.

_____

2 He _____ good food in his kitchen.

_____

3 Now the restaurant _____ ten tables.

_____

4 The boy _____ time to help his father today.

_____

5 The girl _____ time, too.

_____

6 The children _____ fun making salads and setting the tables today.

_____

7 They _____ a good time together in the restaurant.

_____

8 They _____ fun yesterday, too.

_____

Verbs *have, has, had*

Choose the correct word from the chart to complete each sentence.

In the Present	In the Past
have, has	had

1. Joe _____ new running shoes.

2. I _____ new shoes, too.

3. Last week, we _____ old shoes.

4. I _____ a green shirt on.

5. Joe _____ a blue shirt on.

6. Yesterday, we both _____ red shirts on.

7. Last year, we _____ to walk to the park.

8. Now, I _____ skates.

9. Now, Joe _____ a bike.

10. Our friends _____ new bikes, too.

Verbs *have, has, had*

**Read each sentence. If the underlined word is correct, fill in the last
bubble. If not, fill in the bubble next to the correct word.**

1 I <u>have</u> a pet bird.
  ○ has   ○ had   ○ correct as is

2 Now, she <u>had</u> big white wings.
  ○ has   ○ have   ○ correct as is

3 Before, she <u>has</u> little white wings.
  ○ have   ○ had   ○ correct as is

4 The baby bird <u>have</u> closed eyes when it was born.
  ○ has   ○ had   ○ correct as is

5 Now the baby bird <u>had</u> open eyes.
  ○ has   ○ have   ○ correct as is

6 The mother and baby birds <u>had</u> fun now.
  ○ has   ○ have   ○ correct as is

7 The baby bird <u>has</u> little wings now.
  ○ have   ○ had   ○ correct as is

8 It <u>had</u> even smaller wings when it was born.
  ○ has   ○ have   ○ correct as is

ANSWER KEY

Page 5
1. I, . 2. M, I, ? 3. I, !
4. C, I, ? 5. B, I, .
Telling Sentences: I sail my boat in the lake. Bill and I fly the kite.
Questions: May I have a turn? Can Kiku and I play?
Exclamation: I am so happy!

Page 6
1. T 2. C 3. T 4. C 5. Q 6. E 7. Q
1. I, Answers will vary.
2. I, Answers will vary.
3. I, Answers will vary.

Page 7
1. I have fun with my bike.
2. Can I ride to the beach?
3. I found a pretty shell.
4. correct as is
5. Get the shovel.
6. What a mess I made!

Page 8
1. boy, boat
2. brothers, dog
3. girl, grandmother
4. boats, lake
5. Friends, needle, thread, sail
People: boy, brothers, girl, grandmother, friends
Places: lake
Animals: dog
Things: boat, boats, needle, thread, sail

Page 9
1. swing 2. bench
3. children 4. carousel
5. bridge 6. stream

Page 10
1. no 2. yes 3. no 4. yes
1. place 2. person
3. person 4. thing 5. animal

Page 11
1. George Ancona 2. Mexico
3. Jorgito 4. Coney Island
5. Pilar 6. Tio Mario
People: George Ancona, Jorgito, Tio Mario
Animals: Pilar
Places: Mexico, Coney Island

Page 12
1. Sue 2. California
3. Los Angeles 4. Pacific Ocean
5. Tonya 6. Sue Wong
7. Shore Road 8. Austin, Texas
Sentences will vary.

Page 13
1. person 2. place
3. animal 4. place
1. Emilio 2. Orlando
3. Disney World 4. Main Street

Page 14
1. runs 2. wears 3. smacks
4. holds 5. misses 6. waits
7. writes 8. helps
Sentences will vary.

Page 15
1. planted 2. watered
3. weeded 4. discovered
1. present 2. past

Page 16
1. action verb
2. not an action verb
3. not an action verb
4. action verb
1. correct as is
2. rained

Page 17
The following get an X next to them.
2. (Crow) could not get a drink.
3. (The water) rose.
6. (One mouse) had a plan.
Sentences will vary.

Page 18
1. Lin likes to play soccer.
2. Her friends watch her play.
3. They cheer for Lin.
4. Her mom goes to all her games.
5. The coach is very proud of Lin.
6. Elijah plays tennis on Saturdays.
7. The bird built a nest.
8. Sara and Simeon baked a cake.

Page 19
1. telling part
2. naming part
3. not the whole part
4. not the whole part
1. saw the cat go away
2. Then, the bird
3. After a minute, the cat
4. walked back, too

Page 20
2. She, Mom
3. They, The pigs
4. it, a board game
5. They, The pigs and Wendell
6. He, Wendell

Page 21
1. It 2. They 3. It 4. she 5. He

Page 22
1. Ms. Fultz 2. The boy
3. The house 4. The pigs
1. He 2. they

Page 23
1. accordion(s) 2. brush(es)
3. clock(s), watch(es)
4. flower(s), box(es)
accordions, clocks, flowers
brushes, watches, boxes

Page 24
1. sandwiches 2. meals
3. lunchboxes 4. plates
1. boxes 2. dresses
3. coats 4. benches

Page 25
1. sketches 2. foxes
3. correct as is 4. balls
5. correct as is 6. correct as is
7. dresses 8. correct as is

Page 26
1. brown <u>donkey</u>, heavy <u>sack</u>
2. striped <u>cat</u>, two <u>birds</u>
3. little <u>rooster</u>, six <u>times</u>
1. brown, heavy, striped, little
2. two, six

Page 27
1. (animal sanctuary), big
2. (giraffe), tall
3. (girls), two
4. (spots), brown
color word: brown
size words: tall, big
number word: two

Page 28
1. red 2. yellow 3. purple 4. big
5. three 6. little 7. huge 8. Two

Page 29
1. <u>is</u>, present 2. <u>are</u>, present
3. <u>were</u>, past 4. <u>is</u>, present
5. <u>am</u>, present 6. <u>was</u>, past

Page 30
1. is/was, one 2. is/was, one
3. were, more 4. are, more
5. was, one 6. are, more

Page 31
1. past, one
2. present, more than one
3. past, more than one
4. past, more than one
5. past, more than one
6. present, one

Page 32
1. present 2. present
3. present 4. present
5. past 6. past
7. past 8. past

Page 33
1. went 2. goes 3. does
4. did 5. Do 6. go

Page 34
1. goes 2. do 3. does 4. go
5. did 6. went 7. went 8. did

Page 35
2. "That's a great idea."
3. "What should we bring?"
4. "We should bring food."
5. "Yes, let's bring lots and lots
of food."
6. "You're no help at all!"
Answers will vary but should use
quotation marks for speech.

Page 36
2. "What will we do today?"
3. "We could read."
4. "Maybe the sun will come out
soon."
5. "But what will we do now?"
6. "Use your imagination!"
Answers will vary but should use
quotation marks for speech.

Page 37
1. "Let's make a sandcastle," said
Lenny.
2. "Where's the pail and shovel?"
asked Sonya.
3. Sara said, "Maybe Otis can
help."
4. "Do you want to dig?" asked
Lenny.
5. Sonya shouted, "Get some
water!"
6. "Look what we made!" cried
the children.

Page 38
1. <u>aren't</u>, are not
2. <u>doesn't</u>, does not
3. <u>can't</u>, cannot or can not
4. <u>couldn't</u>, could not
5. <u>didn't</u>, did not
6. <u>isn't</u>, is not
1. hadn't, had not
2. don't, do not
3. weren't, were not

Page 39
1. couldn't 2. wasn't 3. aren't
4. can't 5. don't 6. didn't
Sentences will vary.

Page 40
1. aren't 2. isn't 3. can't
4. haven't 5. don't 6. didn't
7. couldn't 8. weren't

Page 41
1. writes 2. meets 3. ride
4. shop 5. closes 6. forget
7. locks 8. bang 9. call 10. hear

Page 42
1. play 2. hides 3. chase
4. calls 5. run 6. stand
7. closes 8. nudges
9. sleeps 10. sleep

Page 43
1. make 2. cuts 3. use 4. glow
5. hang 6. buy 7. picks 8. picks
9. wear 10. sell

Page 44
1. had, past
2. had, past or: has, present
3. has, present
4. has, present or: had, past
5. has, present
6. have, present or: had, past
7. have, present or: had, past
8. had, past

Page 45
1. has or had 2. have or had
3. had 4. have or had
5. has or had 6. had 7. had
8. have 9. has 10. have

Page 46
1. correct as is 2. has 3. had
4. had 5. has 6. have
7. correct as is 8. correct as is